# POEMS: AN HANDFUL WITH QUIETNESS

John Stewart Carter

# POEMS:
# AN HANDFUL
# WITH QUIETNESS

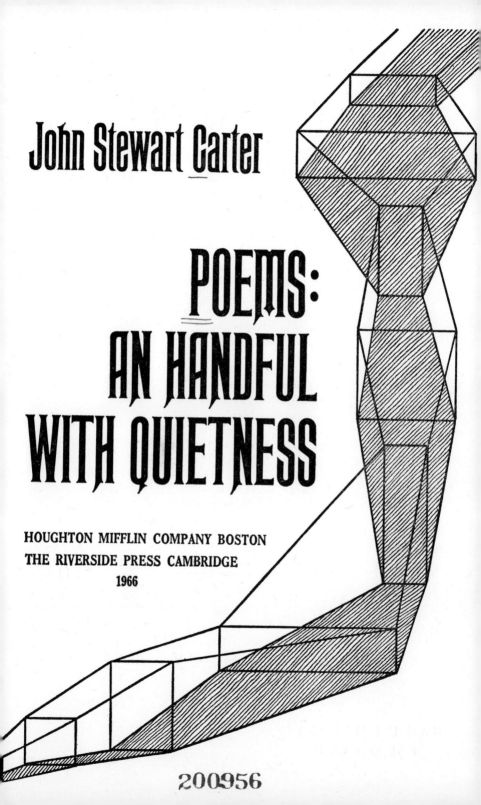

HOUGHTON MIFFLIN COMPANY BOSTON
THE RIVERSIDE PRESS CAMBRIDGE
1966

Certain of the poems in this volume have previously appeared in various magazines as follows:
*American Scholar:* "Child Drawing."
*The Beloit Poetry Journal:* "Assorted Ornaments," "Elegy Written in Montparnasse," "Firenze."
*The Colorado Quarterly:* "Corpse Song."
*Harper's Bazaar:* "In Holy, High Meshed."
*The New Republic:* "No. 6025."
*Tri-Quarterly:* "Amaryllis Belladonna," "Antiphon," "Chinoiserie," "Dimensions," "Elegy Written on the Leaning Tower," "Klavierstück," "Mouse House," "Mr. De Paolis and the Shades" (under the title "The Shirt of Nessus"), "Roma," "Sands Street, Brooklyn," "The Tides of Sea," "Worm Song."
*Voices:* "The Day before the Burgeoning."
*The Western Humanities Review:* "Conversation," "Saturday Night Song."

*Title page decoration by Mitchell Wojtycki*

To Marie, Elizabeth, and Alexandra

*Better is an handful with quietness, than both the hands full with travail and vexation of the spirit.*

ECCLESIASTES IV, 6

# CONTENTS

## ONE
### *Ensanguined dust*

## TWO
### *and they cut down the trees and the shadows*

## THREE
### *carnivorous kind*

FOUR
*in high careen*

FIVE
*a pound of feathers, a pound of lead*

SIX
*beyond similitude*

# ONE

*Ensanguined dust*

# ONE

*Ensanguined dust*

The Time the Ferris Wheels All Stopped

Zoo Song

Assorted Ornaments

Grocery Store

Pompes Funèbres

Great Books

Child Drawing

## THE TIME THE FERRIS WHEELS ALL STOPPED
## (2 RIDES FOR THE PRICE OF 1)

At precisely ten-o-nine,
daylight savings time,
upon midsummer night,
then and there, all over the world,
the Ferris Wheels
(which until then had been turning)
came to slow and silent stop.

The baskets swayed a little,
but the iron bars held tight,
and the carnival sounds
continued on the ground
while the smells arose,
and the lights kept on.
The other people moved around,
big summer ants in glimmer-flow
of going to and senseless fro.

But what a sight
for anyone who looking down
as stars look down
could see the world that night—
a curve of of mountains, valleys, hills,
rivers, lakes, and vast shored seas,
and all the Ferris Wheels at stop,
the baskets swaying
in the summer's breeze:

5

At stop beside the mango tree,
　　At stop beside the pine,
At stop beside the Zuider Zee,
　　At stop in Appenine.


At stop at Legion carnival
　　Sprawled out on pasture lot
Where cotton candy blooms pink clouds
　　Swift swirled from black iron pot.


Oh the barkers barking barkly,
　　The melt of dime in hand,
Where lake of light spilled brightly
　　That golden Samarkand


On clay of inland prairie
　　While circle swayed at top,
And young heart sang not darkly
　　Of Ferris Wheels at stop.

# ZOO SONG

Crocodiles curtsy,
　Alligators reel,
Ostriches, thirsty,
　Suck lemon peel.

Elephants dangle
　Tails and trunks,
One from the back end,
　One from the front.

Trunks pick peanuts,
　Tails flick flies,
Flap ears pendulous,
　Fan slit eyes

Glazed with dark
　Mammalial woes
Herbivorous mammoth
　Ruminative knows.

Zig-zag zebras
　In underwear quiver,
In summer's sun,
　Incontinently shiver.

Pythons polka,
　Monstrous auks
Wingless fly
　While camels gawk

At baboon bottoms,
Sunset tinged,
Simian fundament
Irregularly fringed.

Posturing peacocks,
Eyes in tail,
Screech fowl love
To timorous quail

As dreams uncage
The zoo's derisions,
In Technicolored,
Vistavision.

## ASSORTED ORNAMENTS
## FOR THE CHRISTMAS TREES
## OF THE MIDDLE-AGED
## MADE FROM SCRAPS
## LEFT LYING ABOUT
## THE ELEGIAC MIND

Ribbed
Ferris waist
I one time wore
in nineteen hundred twenty
was buttoned
(yellow bone, not pearl)
by other fingers
down
knit
front
(back, of course, was girls).

Roller towel
rattled from
rickety rack
(blue lines on crash in twenty)
and spun from rung'd back
of pot-pantry door
to which we'd hop
a fresh-scrubbed floor.
(Oh, sun-white maple boards
new strewn
with isolate islands
of slidey
*Tribune*.)

Jap Rose
was a pretty soap
(translucent twenties reeling)

when yellow
bursting
splintered green
in glint
from tile to ceiling,
and bathtub sun
lit glycerin dream
of shattered iridescent gleam
to opulence
of opalene.

Christmas trees
we dragged to lot
(oh twenties, resinous seeping)
and winter blaze
in twilight haze
enkindled to set leaping
balsam light
that licked back night
as curded sky bloomed rose
dissolving hush
where branches flushed
in arch of dark enclose
with black elm fringed
and violet tinged
by mortal boy's suppose.
For there I heard
whirred rush of bird
brush darkness as it came
to snowy land
where still I stand
to fly my kites of flame.

The
Gold Dust Twins
on print-blurred box
(orangely then in nineteen twenty)

washtubs thubbed
and scrubboards rubbed
in corybantic sibling antic.
Polylingual, polyglottal,
gifted young with many tongues
(Teutonic and Romantic)
on back and sides they vowed to banish
grime in German,
French
and Spanish.

Victrolas
were *victrolas* when
(oh echo, hand wound twenties)
in running down
they'd flat to bleat
glint-glitter of bravura
so Galli-Curci'd moo mad bass
for Lakmé's coloratura.
Brass knob
could treble speed and key
and glib quartette
from *Rigoletto*
gabble into gibble shrilled
as daggers sharped
to shrieked stilettoes,
or Schumann-Heink
in squeaked alt trilled
*hoch*-German jabber gibbered
of falsetto *Stille Nacht*
from guttural glabble glibbered.

Warren
Gamaliel Harding died
when mint-bright were the twenties;
we loved his middle name and tried
to think it was historic

that we should watch
from pillared bank
(the capitals were vast and Doric)
his coffin in flagged parlor car
stop at suburban station.
The Legion blew its saddest taps
and we, by invitation,
went into director's room
where a light collation
was served to those so privileged
to represent our nation.
Our mothers wore black hats, black gloves;
our fathers owned bank stock;
outside, non-vested choir sang
of cleft in Ages' Rock.

Hair
Receivers
never held hair
(Haviland lid had hole in twenty)
and things you'd looked for everywhere
often just happened to be there
on account of their being
such very good places
for finding (or putting)
of half-worn shoelaces,

paperless stubs
of purple crayola,
fiber needles
for upstairs victrola,
stamps without any glue
on their backs
(we sent for samples),
ju-jubes, jacks,

rubber bands,
Sen-Sen, aggies or mibs,
pennies, nickels,
(double *van dibs*),
Tinker-Toy sprockets,
garters for socks,
prizes once prized
from Cracker-Jack box,

puzzling pits
of plums and dates,

and fugitive keys
of roller skates.

Dressmaker
ripped, snipped, snapped, and sewed
(treadled twenties whirring)
in sewing room which overflowed
with clack of tongue and shears.
We called her "Mrs. Know-it-all";
she called us "little dears."
While we watched
from back hall stairs,
(not invited in!)
our mother stood
on straight-backed chair,
and she crawled,
mouthing pins.
(Oh cutty scissors —
hers, not ours —
Oh duvetyn, monkey furred!
Oh scarlet velvet evening wrap
with collar crushly shirred!)

Napkin rings
succeeded bibs
(damask twenties sometimes soiled)
and in silver circle held
a past in past itself encoiled.
My brother's had his name, a stork,
his birth date, height, and weight;
it matched the pusher,
spoon and fork
with which he messed and ate;
mine had a Teddy Bear on front,
on back, my name in script;
our mother's we once made ourselves
of birch bark, yarn, and spit;

our father had no need of cramped,
camp-sweated handicraft;
his had been a christening gift
from William Howard
Taft.

Kitchen
Klenzer
teased the mind
of boy on pot in twenties
for cook in kitchen saw herself
complete in repetitious pan
and that cook saw herself again
in still another can

Thus pan
succeeded can
and can
in mirrored pan
bright certitude reflected
which cook
who took
unending look
impassively inspected.

But boy on pot
(as who has not)
the paradox detected
whereby he
reflectively
in gaze from can to can
descried the lot
in pictured pot
of existential man.

For did he not cast glance with pants
dispassionately floorward,

and then expect in retrospect
to look obliquely forward?
Ensanguined dust
forever must
unknot implicit riddle
intrinsic where
extrinsic glare
obscures the mirrored middle.

A GLOSSARY FOR THE YOUNG TO ACCOMPANY "ASSORTED ORNAMENTS"

Ferris waist: This was the trade name for an undergarment worn
by both boys and girls. It was made of fairly heavy, knitted
cotton with a series of buttons to which our trousers (or skirts)
were buttoned. From it suspended tapes which held the remov-
able garters for our stockings. It was not worn on Sundays when
we wore knee-length socks and our black velvet trousers were
fastened by pearl buttons to our blouses (not *shirts*). We gradu-
ated from Ferris waists to B.V.D.'s, belts, and knickerbockers.

yellow bone: I have not seen a yellow bone button in thirty years.
They looked like yellowish soap and had two, rather than four
holes. They were much better for sucking than pearl buttons.
It is, I suppose, sociologically significant that although we were
brought up in what would seem to my own children the most
luxurious and extravagant fashion, some atavistic puritanism
dictated that as long as they did not show, buttons should be
bone.

Jap Rose: This really was a pretty soap, about the color of Vaseline
and translucent in the same way. It did not float. Fairy Soap
and Ivory Soap floated.

roller towel: These, I suppose, have entirely disappeared. I know
that for years our kitchen has been strewn with yards of paper
toweling. They were generally of heavy linen crash and were generally dirty. They were always changed after the floor was
scrubbed.

pot-pantry: There was only one *kitchen cabinet* in the kitchen, which
was never a *cabinet kitchen*. Everything was kept in closets which
were called *pantries*. Actually our roller towel was over the *fireless cooker* upon which we climbed to reach the towel, but if
you want to put a fireless cooker in a poem some time, just try it.

15

white maple: Linoleum did not appear in general use until the mid-twenties. Kitchen floors were always maple, and the woodwork was varnished, not painted, pine.

Gold Dust Twins: This was before the NAACP, and the twins were pickaninnies who cavorted, cartoon fashion, on the front of the orange box. We were utterly fascinated by the instructions. These appeared not only in German script, French and Spanish, but also, it seems to me, in Czech, Swedish, and Dutch. We often had maids who could read them aloud to us to our great delight. Silver polish also contained wonderful directions.

grime: This is a *period* word. I would never use it in such a context for *dirt* today.

collation: This is strictly a *period* word. It meant something provided by a caterer and was perfectly all right for a bank. It would have been considered "meager" at home where it was presumed that, although extra maids might be hired, you were "equipped" to provide any number of guests with "decent" food. Chicken sandwiches and tongue sandwiches — even with the thinnest bread — frappé — which we always called *sloppay* — and "store" *petits fours* would never have been considered anything but a collation.

black hats: These were worn — even in the dead of summer as here — to all funerals and on all *sympathy calls, out of respect.*

Hair Receivers: These were round boxes belonging to *dresser sets.* Sometimes they were ivory; very often, as here, of hand-painted china. By the twenties, since nothing was ever thrown out, they had been retired to children's rooms, guest rooms, and sewing rooms (see below). I think their original purpose was to hold combings of hair. In any case, they matched the powder box (which never held powder) and the trays for combs and brushes. I even remember a vase that matched. This was for hat pins, I was told, and considered it a conspicuous refinement. That it then appeared on the dresser of a new born baby would not have been considered even faintly odd. Of course, it never held hat pins.

upstairs victrola: Almost everything existed in two forms, *upstairs* and *downstairs.* As children we were very seldom downstairs at all, except in the kitchen and in the dining room to eat. There was an upstairs *living room* with its own fireplace arranged for a *gas grate,* a *library table* in the center of the floor, and the *upstairs victrola* — lower case because all phonographs were called *victrolas,* even when they were Brunswicks, as ours was.

dressmaker: The *dressmaker* came to the house one or two days a year, and there was a great flurry of making *over*. Evening dresses in particular were always being made *over*, and I remember three distinct incarnations of our mother's wedding dress. The last, which cleared her knees, was trimmed with swaying, dangling foot-long fringe. The lace at this point was retired to a five-pound candy box across whose padded moiré top were strewn hand-painted forget-me-nots. Her *best* dresses were bought — or made *out* — but last year's best became the new year's second best through the agency of a dressmaker who came to the house.

treadle: The sewing machine was powered by foot. The treadle was large, cast iron, and ornate.

sewing room: All houses had extra bedrooms, the best of which would be called *guest rooms*. The least desirable (by the back stairs) would be called the *sewing room* and furnished with a brass bed, a painted dresser, the sewing machine, and a couple of dining room chairs from *before we were born*.

gift: We *never* said *gift*. We always said *present*, but in this case *gift* rhymes in a halfhearted way with *spit* and has one fewer syllables. Even so, it bothers me.

cook: The woman on the Kitchen Klenzer can was clearly a *cook* and not a *maid*. Maids wore uniforms with long sleeves. Cooks were crabbier than maids.

17

## GROCERY STORE
### (*ca.* 1922)

Tortoise pregnant cat
chalk-swirled-backwards window dreamed
reviL sevlaC dreams

Bananas
hook-hung hinted huge from stalk
Tarantula Death.

Malaga grapes
spilled cork,
Geography, Spain
to grocery-sawdust floor.

Clerks aproned,
pencils eared;
coated owner madam-bowed,
gloved, sniffing teas.

Cheese bell
rose with scale-weight sigh
to dangle years
above all yellow smell.

## POMPES FUNÈBRES
### (*ca.* 1925)

Boy took ham
past gladiola door
where tickless clock stopped
coffin gape.

House at wake
glowed amber eyed
across night street
unsleeping sleep of living boys.

White hearse
windowed nine-year-olds
who sidewalk watched
the dead girl's morning ride.

# GREAT BOOKS
## (*ca.* 1926)

Hardy Boys
sailed sleeping porch
through trees fall-tossed
in cedared eiderdowns.

Tom Swift
copper-spooled oatmeal box,
earphoned sound from air
with crystal poked.

Oil cloth
Dutch girls windmilled
bathroom walls where Silver Skates
sat arm in dike.

Rag picker Fagin
basement-bargained
pursed pennies
lagged to sidewalk crack.

Isinglass
fogged rain as Sherlock Holmes
jump-seated rode
to dancing class.

E. Phillips Oppenheim silk hat
amazed in plopped rise
fatherdead's eyes.

## CHILD DRAWING
### (After Dubuffet)

I will draw a dog, said the child,
and his crayoned inchoate circle
of orange round head, green cat-ears
and brown-pillow body,
but he could not stop his dog from breath
nor wagging of his tail even in his mind,
so he laughed and rooted him to the ground
with purple-stick legs and bird-claw feet,
and he coated the purple-stick legs
with tiny-bubbled spittle from
tumid tip of twisted tongue,
and waxy crayon burst in nose
to many colored smell
with brown of tasted paper swirled.

His tongue now clamped between his teeth,
he filled his circles in, but he could not stop
his dog from breath as his hand moved
beyond the limits of his traces,
though his arm was stiff with trying
and his fingers cramped in agony of nerve,
for he sought form where no form was
nor ever would be.

   Then he drew grass and one tree,
but the tree grew and the grass grew
and there was no use in trying
for they would not stop their growing
and slipped beyond his crayon

and the agony of nerve to grow
with greening smear about the bird-claw feet
and purple-stick legs where still
bright spittle clung.

So he drew a great black sun
which would never set nor grow
and left savage hunks of crayon in gobs
on black sun which did not breathe,
and he saw the terror which his black sun,
his gobbed sun, struck in the body
of his brown dog, and he heard
the grass cry in thin wail of pain
because it had to grow
and the roots of his tree yelled
so that scribbled leaves shook in shriek,
and all the while within his ears
there throbbed the leaden beat and blow
of dark unuttered sob.

He closed his eyes in clutch of dread
and clapped his hands over his ears
so he could not see nor hear the havoc,
but circles grew inside his eyes
to burst and re-form in colorless-color,
and however stopped his ears
he heard the rattle of purple-stick legs
sough in fleshed murmur of reproach.

Through slit of crafty eye he peered
to blur the havoc of his sun —
enormous sun with broken bits
of savage crayon clinging —
and with stealthy tongue, meticulous and cruel,
he bent to pick with lick the biggest;
from folded tip of tongue he pressed it
to tip of rigid little finger.

He dared not look, but he could feel
its black blackness burn the finger's tip
so pain shot through his elbow
and spread to cleave him sore with ecstasy.

Slowly, oh so slowly, slowly —
pain-hard that arm in flex —
he moved his moistened finger
with its black seed
of glistening wax
to tasted paper
to trace
faintest line
from blackest sun
to breath of dog.

# TWO

*and they cut down the trees*
*and the shadows*

# TWO

*and they cut down the trees
and the shadows*

# HISTORIC AMERICA
## (The Funeral Home Is Born)

Willie (like jesus) wept.
Willie was short for Wilma Updyke Ashenbrenner,
which meant that there were great Old English "U's"
on towels and napkins and tablecloths
and all the shining silver all over their shining house,
and she wasn't my cousin or aunt or anything
as she very surely could have been
considering the comings
and goings-on in my family
in nineteen hundred and twenty,
but instead (which is in memory of all the great
Old English "S's" all over our shining house)
she was just a girl, an almost lady,
we all knew who lived in a house
with a wide front porch that swept around to the side
for sitting on in summertime
in summertime dresses with maidenhair fern
and geraniums and VINCA
    (*vincire*, to bind; *vincere*, to defeat)
in hangingbaskets with the moss turned brown
and swing with creaking wicker back and arms
which creaked again on chains
("You make me dizzy, boys")
until the lemonade of cutglass pitcher
clingled sweating in the summertime night.

And then we went home and got undressed on the sleepingporch
and I thought of Willie's grey eyes
and pink-white hands with cameo ring,

the faint, soft down which breathed across her arms,
and her fine, light hair in psyche lifted.
We could hear a beau come then and a ukelele
letthe REST of the WORLD go by
how sweet now
how soft the summertime night
and the creak of wicker swing to sleep
in lap of faintly voices blurred,
but I will never know how I knew,
how I knew that night
that Willie wept like jesus.

I woke to know that she was in our tent.
OUR tent: graham crackercrumbs damp,
smelly cot and sharp greenwood odor
of orangecrate table; stained canvas heat
and grass browned to stubble.
But this was not crying.
Crying we had heard and often.
Willie wept.

And beau's voice burred like biggest bug.
My heart beat so I could not hear with hottest ears
except the sobs I had never heard,
never heard at all in the whole world
and I did not know that they were in the world
or that all the world — mountains, rivers, seas —
could hold them in its arms.
    (Oh innocent age whose children had not heard,
    as ours must daily hear, the sobs of life
    bent from waves of air to sound again
    in every house their mock of deep despair!
    Oh age of final innocence of child who only knew
    that Jesus wept, but weeping had not heard!)
I pressed my face into the screen
and felt the lines that it would make

on forehead and along my nose
which filled with summer dust of blackness to my throat.
Oh, summertime night and small boy looking.
Shadows of maples on moonlight lawn
where night moths fed on webs of dew,
burring beau and Willie weeping.

(So far this is easy for me;
there is mood, and I could let
the soft nostalgia melt in night away,
in summertime night. Recast the lines
to prose, throw away my title and send it all
enambered in gloss to the *New Yorker*.
But there is more, of course,
always there is more,
there keeps on being more,
and this is only part of a part.
Which part of what part
I must try to tell you.)

I saw them come out of the tent and hurry
across the lawn and summer moonlight,
his arm around her waist
her head upon his chest
and the swift little swift steps
of lifting air and wing.
(Ten years later I saw the attitude again
from the gilt-pillared, redplush splendor of a box at
the Paris Opera when two dancers left the stage,
and my mother in a Paquin frock said,
"What are you rubbing your forehead for?"
Well, I knew, for I had smelled the summer dust
of blackness once again,
sharp, exact, and I felt the mark of screen
as I have felt it ever since
when dancers at the ballet strike the pose.

Oh, this is where I should stop remembrance:
the touching tenderness, the little boy,
the grace of memory made motion.
But it was jesuswept, you know I said,
and I wasn't just being cunning.
The little boy was me, the I who speaks today.)

Forty years ago a summertime night
I was alone there, old in the window,
my heart pounding with plots,
my neck on fire with tears which would
not weep themselves nor melt away,
my tongue dry with knowledge,
a knowledge I knew had to be mine alone.
I shut my brother out, and I didn't tell him a thing.
Not a thing. Though he lay in the bed next to me
and had a right to know and see
because it was his tent too.
And his world
and the world to which he must come.
So I went to wide-eyed sleep
as love crumbled to graham crackercrumbs on hot pillow.
I was on my own.
Oh was I ever on my own!

Right away, the next day,
I began to call Willie,
"Willie-the-weeper," and everybody else did, too,
and we chanted it around the houses and yards
and in the stained canvas-heat of our tent
where the grass was browned to stubble,
but no one else knew why except me.
I would steal a glance at Willie as
we used the words in that past time
but she never flinched and I began
to think I'd dreamed the night that Willie wept,

but once she caught my looking
and I knew
and I swelled with power
and I saw fear alive
but it did not matter
because I wasn't any more alone.
I had Willie with me.
She knew and took my guilt with hers.
I could feel it lump between her little breasts.

Back there in time I can hear the littleboy voice
that said, "I guess I'd better take my tent down now" —
  (ALL RIGHT YOU SHALL HAVE THE REST OF IT.
  I HAVE HAD IT FOR MANY YEARS, WHY NOT YOU?) —
"Maids and things use it, you know."
I wasn't struck dead. Nothing happened.
Nothing at all except that life
began to dilute at once what I had said:
Willie turned and fled from the porch
into the upstairs house where we
had never been but where we knew
nightgowns hung in lingered haze of gauzy smell
from hooks behind closed closet doors
and Kotex stood in blue box on linen closet floor.
"You shouldn't tease Willie so," her mother said,
(the placid voice drifts back through years)
"She's nice to you, you know, and it's just silly
that Willie-the-weeper business."
And the wicker swing creaked on chains
and if Willie wept across her bed
I could not hear her on the porch.

That fall Willie married Tom,
Tom-Tom-the-Piperson we called him
because that was his name, Mr. Piperson,
and he hadn't been to any college at all
and he did not belong to the club,

and he wore things in his buttonhole
and his father was dead and so was his mother
and he was a ROMAN and an undertaker.
   (I have to explain to people who came in
later than I did and the people I'm talking about
that in those days funerals were parlors,
at the very most, and never HOMES
and the corpse's place was in the parlor
of his own LATE HOME, so that undertakers
were not pillars of society but just had
a kind of STORE with two big BOSTON ferns
and a rolltop desk with a green light over the desk
coming home after charliechaplin
in the store front where the medical student studied
until he went BACK
and NIGHT BELL).

   (And I will also have to explain about Willie's father:

| | |
|---|---|
| the Williefather was | prosperous |
| which was above being | well-fixed |
| but not so nice as | comfortable |
| or | well-off |
| and after that | |
| we did not mention it | |
| at all because we did not like | |
| to say | rich |
| and only people less than | well-fixed |
| were allowed to say | wealthy |

AND THOSE WERE THE RULES
And if you do not know the rules
there is no sense playing.)
But Willie married Tom Piperson.
Indeed she did, that very fall,
and they got married in the Presbyterian Church.
   (The assumption was the Presbyterians and perhaps the

Episcopalians would avail themselves
of Tom's services when they had mortal need
and since he was a ROMAN, the Romans would, too.
Which was a very happy arrangement
and very common in those days.)

But at her very own wedding, Willie wept;
not like jesus, but with real tears, if you can imagine,
and if you can't, pray do so at once
because here is a veil
and some tears
and the choking scent of flowers
and the organ is so beautifulsad
with chickensalad in the churchparlor
provided by the ladies of Circle 9,
for those were the rules.
But it was commented upon, oh yes commented upon
that Willie Updyke Ashenbrenner with the Roman business
had Circle 9 provide the chickensalad
instead of the club with lobster Newburgh as well
and an awning to the curb at church
AND at home and their own maids JUST
in the bedrooms at home and the club's maids
and the club's steward all over the DOWNSTAIRS
and palms and a string quartet.
Oh commented upon certainly in nineteen-twenty
when Willie shone with tears behind her veil,
and I, a little boy, stood on a patch of grass
browned to stubble where once our tent stood,
and watched the Ashenbrenners come home
without their only Willie.

Willie, pretty Willie, went to live above a store
    (for those were the RULES and Willie knew the RULES)
and there they stayed until her father died
which did not take very long.
Tom-Tom-the-Piperson made all the arrangements then

for which the house was well suited,
and I saw Willie weeping again
but I did not even think of Jesus.
Some politicians came to the funeral
(which was certainly a departure
although not so much of a departure
as if the Williefather had been          comfortable)
and the handwriting
was on the wall
was on the wall, all right,
and when the Williemother went to live in Pasadena
they moved right into the house
from the flat above the store
and they took over the house
and they did not go to the store
any more
and right there
on a regular street
with regular people living on it,
which was AGAINST ALL THE RULES
the ROMANS
and a little later
the PRESBYTERIANS
no longer lay in the parlors
of their own LATE HOMES.
      (Lang, lang did the ladies sit i' the kirk
      wi'their fans i' their hands —
      fans with assorted scenic wonders
      on thin cardboard face
      a greenwood stick
      and a muddy print of the Ashenbrenners' house
      on the back with a legend in Old English:
            A Residence of Distinction
            Completely at your Disposal
              In Time of Need
            Piperson's Funeral Home

Now they lay in the Ashenbrenners' parlor
when they were dead
and pall bearers and politicians
smoked cigars on the porch
where no baskets hung
nor swing-chain creaked
nor VINCA drooped
    (*vincire,* to cling; *vincere,* to vanquish)
nor geraniums bloomed
upon the summertime night.

And so we moved away and everyone moved away
and they tore down all the houses
and cut down the trees and the shadows
and covered the lawns with buildings
which stopped the night moths' mouths,
and only the Ashenbrenners' is still there
waiting for us to arrive for one last time
in creaking wicker basket;
only our throats will be coated
with the black summer dust
of screens once breathed.

## DINNER PARTY

### (*ca.* 1920)

Wine rinsed
empty glasses rose;
violets drowned thread-stemmed
in tepid finger bowls.

Cigar smoke
choky blue-layered air
as ice cream melted messed
guttered gold pagoda'd Spode.

Dr. Dentons
crept huddling giggles
damask tentward hunching
haunches waiting

wilted pom-pommed
Daniel Greens of ache-foot maids
with Swedish jabber,
japanned trays

to rump tap
pong up back stairs shushed
to quick-smoothed bed and wisp-haired kiss
whispering smell

of third floor rooms
where underwear had long limp strings
and cotton puckered over
bone-clamped breasts.

Then diamond laughter
cut glass rose to bell with burst
in inmost lonesome ear
the sleepiness of warmy tears.

TOKEN CANDLES
FOR THE BIRTHDAY CAKES
OF THOSE APPROACHING FIFTY

Silk umbrella
slit in rise
from terra-cotta jar
to slanting rain.

Polar bear
on ice-card ice
asked Red Grange college boy
with black iron tongs.

Tortoise shell
bloomed fingered ostrich plumes
to cover knees in opera box.

Furrier-windowed ermine
taxidermist fanged
bead-eyed death of mink.

Cousins spat
long Sunday afternoons
down clothes chutes
into giggly eyes.

Measle-face
window-waved, stuck out tongue,
thumbed nose; shade shot up.
Arm retrieved.

Electric charging
sputtered coach house blue;

pitched pine stairs
led you know where.

Wet slick dog
shivered sunlight drops to grass
forgiving trembled backyard bath.

Beaded bag
snagged boy-bit nails
in satin fumble slipping
fingered dime.

Nevaleek
patched pumped bike tire;
upsidedown whirred wheel spun
spoking sun.

Razor strop
bit frantic backside
mutinous constrict
yelped raging tears.

Hunchbacked
peddler back porch spooned
hottest horseradish wooden pailed
to jar.

# KLAVIERSTÜCK

Krakauer upright oak as stone,
felts moth-sponged then mat as shreds
upon the white-pine clapper pegs
while hammers' amber tears of glue
were wept to final, brittle, varnish chips.
  (The blind tuner warned
  before he left
  at morning's end,
  tools in wet-green plush
  of slotted case,
  white cane ferrule
  tapping cement doom
  down sidewalk sunlight
  felt, not ever seen.)

The linen strips, age-stiffened folds,
retract not now in dim percussive haunt
of *Für Elise* or other *albumblätter*
chubby fingered by the hair-bow girl
in Mary Cassatt light of storm
not come but coming-sudden soon
when last lace curtain, stiffened plucked
from pins of soft-wood stretcher,
summer billowed past the Boston fern
in salt-glaze jardiniere and loosed
to winds of room blue ice-card eagle —
claws clutched lightnings, beak held flag —
a hundred pounds to parlor rug.
  ("You should take good care,"

blind tuner said.
"The harp's still good.
They do not make them now,
nor will they any more.
You cannot sound against
unseasoned matchboard
in so little room.")


But cast harp cracked at Krakauer heart
and mastodonic reach of frozen keys
yellowed into ivory silence then
in other rooms on other streets
I have not seen except with eyes
beneath slab top become memorial shelf
to hold a jesus-awful plaster Christ
and picture of the deep-loved dead
who died betimes and dimming now must stare
blinder than the tuner tapping far away.
    ("It all depends," he said,
    "in knowing what
    you've got to deal with."
    Finger changed chromatic
    chords in rise,
    and trembly hand would tighten pitch
    with clicking wrench
    constricting throat with ache of sound.)


Then steam-craned claw peeled
brownstone back and left piano
slanting nut-house high above
the rubbled quake where step-gut stairs
climbed bannistered with slant
to fourth floor flat, last tenants
housing project fled, and this memorial
amid wallpapered picture squares.

(I sat on bench
with breathing tuner then
to watch him move
and thought that I could stare
without his knowing
when swift his hand became
claw taloned on my arm
to thrust it hard
between enormous heat
of legs quick clamped
in spastic rock
of high-pitched giggle
shuddered to release
I did not understand.)

Acrosonic spinet now
yields not fumbled *Für Elise*
  (thumb under, three, four,
  one, sharp-the-"F," then three, four,)
and tuner is not blind
nor taps with metronomic cane
into sunlit dark away
  ("G"-not-"A," and three, four,
  pedal up, and triplets come).
Now drones electric ice to clouded cold
not cut from blue-flamed depths of winter pool
when front-bay eyrie eagle fled
  (bring-up-the-bass, and three, then four,
  the little finger takes the "B")
and nine years old I saw from bend
in stair the caller-girl I did not know
and moment wait on thunder.

What note was caught by picture wire,
plucked to sing from wall?
Had I forgot this resonance,

this bloody Orpheus new come
all harpy-torn from Hebrus stream
to hum through toilet-papered comb?
Must eye, vesiculate with sound, now hear,
the labyrinth of ear entune to sight,
the trembling fingers so re-chord on keys
slick spread in plastic denture-grin
the storm in wait, the thin echoic rue
as bright tin wail from membranous kazoo?

# THREE

*carnivorous kind*

# THREE

## *carnivorous kind*

Worm Song

*Amaryllis Belladonna*

Beach Weed

Madam, May I Present?

Mr. R. Browning-Bishop

Psalter

Saturday Night Song

Landscape with Figure

Dimensions

Epigram

A Room within the Palace

The Day before the Burgeoning

# WORM SONG

I would not stay
a single day
were love not still around.

I'd spend my breath
achieving death
and hasten to compound

my clay with dust
where teams the lust
that seethes within the ground.

There root impales
the flesh that fails
to live at love forever

and ciliate binds
carnivorous kind
to vegetable endeavor.

Imperious need
of rose I'd feed
to tendril tender heart

and welcome spawn
beneath green lawn
of worm in private part.

*Amaryllis Belladonna*
(Where Strumpeted Eyes Slack)


Implausible in pot
  protuberant bulb
    of leafless amaryllis
      naked blurts
        fantastic phallus
          upside down in air
                      where
bursts a finial dream
  taut with vein
    in nightmare mock
      of purple blued past ache
        to orgiastic bloom
          of trumpet lily
                      strumpeted
with gorgeous tropic rot
  of jeweled slough
    from scale-coiled snake
      which spits through stalk
        to streak the petaled lips
          with venomous dyes
                      eyes


moist hermaphroditic
  public love
    and mucous pistil smeared
      with yellowed wealth
        of pollen strewed
          from pulvinate sac
                      slack

in wet wither
shriveled tassel leaks
tear from tip
and runny terror seeps
through fingers dilate
after soft remove.

# BEACH WEED

Dazzle weed in clutch of swift-shift sand
  eye glut with hybrid opulence of rose
  deep at feed in earth's compost enclose
  where hairy fingers tentacled demand
suburban rot as gleet of long-spent gland.
  Blown great with greed, graft flower glows
  with spectral glair from scion stalk that grows
  to callused stock as ghost of man unmanned.

Guzzle weed the runneled piss of boys
  in rainbow arch at noon of cycled day
  above the sparse geometry of bloom
while spectrum of its bubble spume alloys
  with cling of silver splotch the gold drenched dune
  sun-parched of dews that thirsts of dawn allay.

## MADAM, MAY I PRESENT?

(Mirabell to Millamant after the
Close of *The Way of the World.*)


This, beloved, is Love:
Madam, may I present?
I want you to get to know each other.
You have much in common, you two,
prone as you are, occupants
of the same delicious, seamy bed,
sharing the same most un-prone man,
breathing the same commingled breath.

All right, it is a quondam sin, a primal shame
that people have, as you say, to behave
just like this. It really is.
Any other ridiculous way
would serve as well to point the paradox:
But those are Sartre's other people,
implausible paupers in little hells
of their own limited devising,
while we, a handsome pair, have Love,
a rich, importunate guest as chaperone
to make plausible even the look of it.

You twist my words and limbs:
a smear of truth, of love, that is —
thank you, thank you,
my most happily prurient prude —
cannot redeem the whore, the meretrix,
the mere artifact who can
a sad and specious innocence assume —
they do, really they do —

or grin with grimmest grinning grin
in fatal expiation — fatal to Love, that is —
of the posture's low absurdity.

But we, bedizened — yea festooned
with lilting laughter — greet our guest
with courteous coquetry the ribald while
we plot a phoenix immolation to beguile
our grimmest grin to body's silent smile.

## MR. R. BROWNING-BISHOP ORDERS
## A COLLAGE FOR CHRISTMAS

I'll have a sky as blue as a marble, please.
Mix it up so that I can see. A couple of clouds, too.
Very unreal and again like the marble —
a glassy pitted, chipped, and just left over
from a life by accident. It lies now,
cold blue and white, among the collar stays
and lockless keys strayed to a little box,
a round enamel coffin on top a walnut bureau.

Very nice, that blue. It looks as if the sky
had entered the sea to make it bluer.
I can remember the sky doing that,
aching with light and rising again
from the stillness and the salt,
clouds lapping to foam above a foamless sea
so that the sky was clear in the sea
and the sea clear in a sky
trembling with light.

Just daub it on. Let the card show through in places.
Right. Exactly right. You have a sure hand
for these things, but I didn't think you could ever get
a blue like that. But no one will notice,
now that it's on, unless he remembers.

Next I'd like an angel, an angel
with society column skirts — herewith —
cut from *The New York Times.*
Let the glue seep to brown the print,

and gore the skirt with theater stubs —
also herewith from bright enameled coffin:
Post-Deb (ORCH) Pledges (NOV. 9) Troth
Ex-Prince (RO)ton Pilot (WF) to Wed.

Now paint me a face, brown-eyed and round,
the eyes looking up to that blue with all
the awful wisdom of vacuity.
I will make the phrases you must paint.

We'll have picture-wire arms,
but splay such wire to bloodless sinews,
veins like colored chart behind
the closet door of doctor's office.
Fray now the ends below hard-knotted wrist
to hands while hands fan to fingers —
stinging wisps of finger to pierce and cling
in all directions. Wonderful. Wonderful.
Her mouth is all greed and her eyes look up
to the sky and clouds on such a day
as I so well remember.

Éloise will be her name, Éloise;
and we'll make her hair of new wood-shavings.
There is nothing so blond as new wood-shavings.
And Éloise, Éloise was satin blond,
nostalgically blond and silken her hair.
In curls it will fall, and pale, pale blond
over her cardboard breast,
for Éloise was satin blond;
nostalgically blond and silken her hair.

Now out of the sky I want you to paint
Murillo cherubs, four in a line,
naked, buttock-pink but with red fingernails
thumbing their noses at her. Her, my Éloise,
Éloise, nostalgically blond.

All across the bottom where it needs something heavy
write "Noël" in thick broad letters
the red of the cherubim's fingernails.
My angel's feet can be the dieresis.
The same color again; most exact.
Careful. Most careful. When it's right, it's heavenly
against the glassy's blue of sea.
A celestial impudence befitting —
oh befitting, befitting, befitting —
the cacophony of my angel,
my Éloise.

There remains to write my name
in childish, cursive hand,
a halo for my Éloise, Éloise.
My Éloise nostalgically blond whom I
so well remember.

# PSALTER

*(The initial letters are of considerable interest,
being formed of jeweled snakes, splendidly gilt.)*
— catalogue description

Ah the snakes, the snakes St. Patrick drove
from Ireland's holy shore when time was mist,
slither-crawled the saltest seas through storms
whose lightnings burned a path through the channel waves
black-edged with fury foamed from green-dark depths.

Beached they lay a moment stunned on rocks —
shale slabs sucked and flung with random
splintered shock to slate and shingle shore —
as cold weeds lifeless strewn until the sun
drew glint of scales to fishy glitter bright.

Inheritors of Eden, driven thus,
made way to fens and bogs, lay coiled in rest
at root of cattails stiff with brackish rise,
slicked fern, and loosed the silent rust of spore
in flake from underside of uncurled frond.

Insinuate with primal dreams they drew
their lengths along the meads thick meshed with thatching
roots of yellow daisy, lupine, clover, wort,
and drank the song from thin-shelled eggs of larks;
bloodless sucked warm blood of marrowed mice.

But mouse and lark content not snake at range
intent on man within the abbey gates
where holiness of days must bloom with riot
when sleep uncloisters veins in afferent night
and drowsy balm of ooze grows cold to touch.

Memorial fingers now must limn at noon
such snakes upon the *Ave's* gilty *A*.
Jeweled so with heather-lavender of hills,
coiled serpentine in sinuous love they'll hiss
through forked vermillion tongues redream of kiss.

# SATURDAY NIGHT SONG

Cressid, harlot, hot musk shed
and thrashed in roil of tented bed
on stubbled plain of troubled Troy
to deep delight of Trojan boy.

Beyond the terms of Pandarus' sale,
he pleasured pleasure to entail
heart and loin in jocund act,
conjoining fancy, rigid fact.

But now we must, my Troilus lad,
make do with less than somehow sad
Cressida, avuncularly sold
on storied plain in realms of gold.

How hear in specious moan of strumpet,
while downstairs jeers a jukebox trumpet
lipping last of jittery dime,
primal song, not purchased whine?

Or lie like Eliot's numbed clerk,
who dillied gray-cat in the dark,
and see in dallied doughy doxy
enigmatic Cressid's proxy?

Oh wisely spendthrift Troilus spent
himself and heart in musky tent
and needed not face neon dawn
when stubbled plain became dewed lawn.

# LANDSCAPE WITH FIGURE

Quiet flowed with light along
the swollen river's spreading shore
and the insistence of the rain
bleared with dawn to dripping hush
as sight seeped muting sound.

Aslant, a willow leaned in blur
of scarcely leaving leaves across
the murk-drenched margins of the night
while silver washed the trembling hour
to yellowed smear of faintly greening spring.

In rush the rain-wet stream poured
tarnished fullness through the clayey bank.
Grey bled brown of new-torn earth
and black, cruel-twist boughs of winter trees
were borne in toss of songless flood.

The man left the window then
turning to the greed-dark room.
He gathered grief about his shoulders
as if it were a shawl and he
a woman in need of warmth at throat.

Pain and the sound of rain returned
as blind fingers clutched clench
of wooly fullness which was not there.
Rot-soft the agony began its ooze once more.
"Sissy" was the word numbed mind gutted bore.

# DIMENSIONS
## (Suburban Showing)


"This is where I came in," he said
and footed through the stumbled row
of feet, brushing rigid knees
politely spread.
                    Ahead in South Pacific
Vistavision two-yard lips
agape met gleaming two-yard lips
wet with Technicolor wanting.

He turned and slanted up the aisle
in plod of middle age intent
on cigarette.
                    Stereophonic
bongo drums, muted trumpets,
catgut soar of violins
fiddled with the plumping loins
of ranch-type steadies teenish sprawled
by Friday night in movie dark
where tinier tongues lick popcorn crumbs
in salter, small similitude
from hotter, buttered mouths.

# EPIGRAM

*Lines discovered on the reverse of a library call slip*
*attached to a blotter, once scarlet, now pink with*
*age, cut in the shape of a Valentine heart.*

Can blotter hearts blot out the pain,
And in the blotting blot the stain
From out my heart which will not clot
But bleeds, and bleeding then bust blot?

# A ROOM WITHIN THE PALACE
## (A Dialogue for Brothers)

"Oh the old man had much to do, tearing
out his eyes like that and leaving us
to stare at one another here in emptied Thebes,
our sockets so alive with famished shame
that horror feeds on horror to englut
its own increase."
                    "Cry not out nor bellow.
We are not a chorus of citizens to moralize,
nor of women to weep. We're offstage, you and I —
a room within the palace —
alone in unrecorded history
the while our father falters forth uncertain
on the stony path to distant sacred grove
of high Colonus."
                    "There he'll smell again
the pine, long needled, coned, and with his fingers
crush the berried cedar's woody lace
to fume. Sticky then his fingers as
at our begetting. Will he remember?
The heart at aromatic pause with love
before its stop?"
                    "Come gentle, gentle Polynices.
My cheek I'll wet against the slither
of your tears still salt but cold — cold, cold
with presage of that after-time that is
our doom. Your hand I'll finger thus and lip
the nervy sinews back to clutching life
although they will contract upon my throat
to stop my lungs."

"Such sorrow must not be.
Sophocles himself has not dared to give it tongue.
Here, feel my heart at piston thud beneath
the useless-nippled breast taut-fleshed with woe.
Let it teach yours to beat congest with rage
and not to tatter to unprincely rags
unfit for chill of dreams our father has
predreamed for us today."
                              "I had not thought
of that. We've not slept yet, nor known the night.
What dream, think you, our father dreamed
in the hot delivery of my seed from out his loins?
Or your? Jocasta juicy, he at rut.
There were different dreams at our engenderings
and yet we are of one flesh sprung."
                              "Hot King
Oedipus the Just, the Sage, the Kind.
We could tell them a thing or two, you and I
who never yet Jocasta loved but always him.
His strength, his laugh, the skim of stones he'd throw
with dazzling muscled ease to ripple echo
far, far out in open sunlit waters.
The piercing wonder of the whistle he could shrill,
fingers pulling lips to white so dogs —
or we — would bound with adoration to
his side."
                    "He never called but that we came.
And yet I remember you and me and him
in mystic circle on a beach. Our legs astride
we mocked his very peeing —
golden, hot, strong, copious as a horse;
ours white, puny, thin. But even so,
we were befouled by trick of shifting wind.
He laughed at us as apes, but did not say
to us as men, 'Choose your ground, my boys,
piss only with the wind.' Such things a man
should teach his sons."

"It is too late now.
He is himself besplattered and has torn out his eyes.
Were they his own eyes he feared or ours?
That day we giggled at our shame, sons of a king.
Today we are denied and will be denied hereafter.
Our sisters' eyes, not ours, will see him stumble.
Our sisters' arms will bear his holy weight
While he, intent upon a legend, leaves
us here within a palace peopled but
with shadows as if after long disuse."

"The shepherds' fires bloom in dusk of hills,
but still the sea holds what is left of light.
Cerulean — the old man never used
so ornate a word, nor I 'til now.
It has the ache in it we need tonight
although the selfsame sea has washed our shores
with azure dusk at every twilight we
have known in this most beautiful of isles.
The lustrous marble cliffs retreat to ghost
the fading shimmer of the masty pines.
The moment quivers and soon is done.

So it is with us. We could have made
a kind of death tonight in one another's arms
beneath the blaze of August stars,
the sough of pines in threnody the while.
The lap of tideless sea would know no pause
nor nightingale constrict one note of song
at our surcease before the flutes of dawn
piped sweet in fields their then unheard aubade."

"Bemused by breath breathed soft to tears of song,
these the latest words of love we'll speak,
for we are sons of him — half poets but
protagonists by blood within ourselves.

On high hot splendor of our Grecian noon
the massy cedar doors swing wide on cue
and we must enter greaved with figured gold —
razored, scented, curled, in mask behind
our maskings masks quite masked."

                                          "Our tendoned thighs
we will annoint to muscled marble sheen'd
by balmy oils he onetime bloody prized
in hot foray across an icy stream.
Our breasts will blaze with wolves that fang in leap
bright suns embossed on interlocking suns,
and folds of royal scarlet skirt our loins
as cock crest glows from graven helm
in toss of darkling green that is the depth
of shimmered blue in plumes of wettest black.
Though trumpets will outbrass the quavering reed,
we spend the rainbow spindrift of his tragic seed."

# THE DAY BEFORE THE BURGEONING

The day before the burgeoning
the weighted heart must waiting bear
the green of brown in gum-wet bud
at resinous pause in ocherous air.

The day before the blooming
the waiting heart must weighted know
the burden of such amorous rise
as moists the bough with augurous flow.

The day before the flowering
the burgeon-burdened heart will loom
from days before the blossoming
the days beyond the bloom.

# FOUR

*in high careen*

# FOUR

*in high careen*

FOUR

(*Le temps retrouvé*)


Forsythia
on a blear gray day
showered tissue bells
and bluely gas would hiss
at thermostatic purr
to presage warmth of flow.

Tomatoes
fingered grit
with picnic sand
slithered slick formica top
where others ate with silver spoons
of rind-bright melons wet.

Palm fronds
click fibrous-febrile clatter-clack
through varnished el train windows
opened once in high careen
so many sudden springs ago.

Dachshund
nuzzling now
through loose spread lap
(trembling soon may cease)
seeps softly heat
to crepey loin.

# THE TIDES OF SEA

The tides of sea enfold the earth
and move as moon makes dim demand
with unslaked ache of mortal thirst
about the fertile, teeming land.

Within the wooded folds of earth
I yet may find such magic spring
which at my dearest touch will make
the gladed valleys gladly sing.

Then lid-closed eyes will dream redream
beyond the moon-struck tidal might
which wastes the shore of fertile land
and sounds salt dissonance of night.

# ACROPHILE

The cat
when dogged
by actuality
will claw a philosophic flight
to utmost crotch
of tree

where he
with eye befogged
denies causality
and washes from a slant of light
with lilting lick
and quickest flick
of apodictic tongue
the dust of vast
absurdity.

Lest we
unwisely should infer
a pusillanimous fright
implicit in percipient flight
he wraps
in prodigality of fur
an existential purr
and so enjoys
felicity
of height.

# GRAND BAROQUE

If you in still proud marble
might so imprisoned be
thus to live immortal
and not to die with me,

gone would be your laughter,
blank your eyes would stare,
cold your breast's warm swelling,
stone your soft black hair.

If I in sweetly singing
might once your grace set free,
transposing breath to music
so you'd not die with me,

gone would be your silence,
tongued to chattering art,
fled that soundless music
which comprehends my heart.

Nor porphyry, nor any song
can catch high-startled cry
when new-amazed in double joy
a single death we die.

Unnerve these arms; unword this tongue;
in shared mortality
immortal calm pervades all sense
when you so die with me.

## SONNET FOR SAINT VALENTINE

Not cynic yet, my sentimental saint?
Nor closed your chiseled eyes, nor deaf'd your ears,
But still untaught by Time's slow seeping taint
The lesson of the repetitious years?

You hear the fatal lies that quicken pain,
That catch the throat, that tear new life apart —
For flesh to flesh is then conjoined in vain
When stops the steady flow from heart to heart.

You see — however dim your vigil light —
The eyes that once in tender fullness shone,
Now blinded by the unwept tears of night,
Bereft of pride, betrayed to barren bone.

   If you, my saint, can thus deny love's woe,
   Once more I too would so forget to know.

# ROCOCO

Might I inter in one sepulchral urn
The winnowed dust and fine compounded clay
That living once drew quick its breath to yearn
And loving lived its onetime splendid day,

No mournful requiem then would I intone
To sing our souls to all embracing rest,
When we in ashy silence lie alone,
And both our hearts are stilled within one breast.

No pious epitaph would mark that bier,
No acid line would etch that chill dark lead
To ghost our story to the crescent year
And weep us so among the crumbling dead,

For dust with dust commingled, dear, would lie,
And being dead, we'd no more live to die.

# SOUND AND SENSE

(Mr. De Paolis at a Solemne Musicke)

"The copulation," wrote Richard Strauss
to von Hofmannsthal, "is in the orchestra."

As cymbal uttered far away
disturbs the calm of nearer air
impinging mind with memory
of odor breathed from golden hair,

so cadence heard in murmuring wind
will drench the sense with trembling light,
freeing form from wreath of past,
and sound a face to yearning sight.

As reedy phrase of aching flute
dissolved to faint remembered gleam
imbues the lip with taste of breast
and tongues the heart to rue of dream,

so touch can quicken at the sound
of strings bowed long ago
and hands and arms and marrowed bones
in ecstasy of knowing know.

The final resonance of sense
reverberates in the pouring out —
but oh, my love, may we prolong
the echo felt before the shout.

# THE MELT OF NUNS

I onetime saw in river rise
clay-swirled chicken coops,
dead wet hens, a billowed cock,
drowned cats, dogs, line-strayed sheets,
and empty pillowcase balloons —
domestic debris more wet with drench
of new-slant rain than melt of mountain snows.

I stood to watch in freaking wind
the dusk train pass the trestled bridge
to other bank where hills began
to smudge in distant rise —
car on car on car with swishing jolt,
lit windows furious with the icy wash of sky
sluiced to glass in fall to flood.

For some reason — it does not matter now
nor has recurrent dream explained —
the engine comes to steamy stop.
(The watchers are not always dreamed
the same, but very likely now
my father, red-haired though dead
for many brown-eyed years, is there.)

We clutch wet hands together as we stand
mired in uncertain soil
as if to will the engines strength to pull.
In dream — and then — the last might
is gathered from our hearts and wrenched,

gasped with spasm into chug which draws
from muscled flex its very thrust.

In moment's hand-clasped stop
big with wills in urgency conjoined,
I see I saw two nuns inside the train,
little girl-doll kneeling on a roomette berth,
habits awry, veils fallen back,
noses snouted white to windowpane,
contorted lips breath-spittling glass.

They have no hands for busyness
of beads and all their weight is thrown
forward to face in nerve-numbed crush,
for neck looks snapped and only held
to body sack by starched bandage bound
from throat in loop to white coiffed head
adangling puppet up.

Looking out to river havoc spilled,
their eyes are closed in agony of dread;
they cannot see the drowned, domestic dead,
the sheets clean washed of dribbled life
now bloat with monstrous flood that bears
the silt of unknown hills alive with rush,
or those who wish them to a chaster shore.

Release of chug snorts spew of steam in hiss
as icy window swill distorts white smear
and eyeless flows with melt of unveiled nuns
dissolved in moving light that sickles swath
towards clay-sogged feet constricting toes
in swift reflexive curl that clings
to handclasped shores of rising spring.

# DAWN SONG

Naked.
        awake in sleep,
                between silked mirrors,
                          at a slant
                      Reflecting.
           only darker blur,
      of bodies,
far away
Tender.
      sleep-tender,
          roused each to each,
                  to know at drowse veined
                              flesh
                              Fleshed.
                in all loosed crush,
      of fingered hairs,
fingering
Mouthed.
      and many arms,
            to throb,
               to moist
                  to flow.

Trillium.
        lingers white
                as pollen blown by night
                                from stars
                                      Incredible.
                        eyes look full on eyes
           and hands now hands
clasp thanks
Song.
        sings in dawn
                so gladly sweet with echoed dream's
                                    undreaming
                                    Joy-sad
                    in silked mirrored haze
           each drowses so to each
from one
Lone.
        not lonely reach
                to draw with roots
                        from heart
                              new sleep.

# BEFORE THE SHEPHERDS CAME
## (Stanzas for St. Joseph's Day)

Who cleaned the stable forking straw
brushed hollowed gold with sheen of silk
by flicker of uncertain lantern's gleam —
shadowed, shadowing the arched back
with interlace of looming rood
upon the sooty weight of beams?
    Did the woman sleep?

Who rhythmic footed gently dogs
carnivorous at steamy sniff
from scarlet blood of birth new spilled
in mess and moist — now red, now black,
enclaved from glistened shift of light —
as slick to weightless lift of hay?
    Did the woman drowse?

Who heated water, sponged the unshaved,
rheum-clot hairs, and bathed the child
delivered from parenthesis of thighs?
Put him to breast more hungry than
the wizened lips reluctant to take teat
and suck the dug to eat of life?
    Did the woman smile?

Who held not-swaddled boy by heels
and gave the verifying glance?
Cut essential cord and tied
the slithery knot with calloused fingers
quick with quiet urgency

of unaccustomed task assumed?
    Did the woman cry?

When eyes amazed with pain beseeched
the tenderness of other eyes
redrinking anguish welling there,
whose hand bore imprint of the woman's nails?
Did she look to him with private love
that every man must have to live,
before the shepherds came?

# A CHANGE OF BELLS

## (To Be Rung at Christmas)

*verb* (n) A word which
affirms or predicates

in silver act of newly Is
bright heart was born to Was
and lay in had-been cool of straw
untarnished yet by smutch of does

by Am begot in sole beget
(oh loneliness of that begetting)
on only Was of all to be
enChilded child with choice besetting

subjunctive were of if and wish
the should-have-been the doubt of had
in smoke of frosty breath dissolve
on chilly morn by Is made glad

in want beyond the dangled star
the song to sky of our behold
will ring a change to peal of Is
for tumult rung from soar of told

so wisemen came in come to give
abiding shepherds ring glad rang
the only Is of Am to sing
the had-to-be which angels sang

# FIVE

*a pound of feathers,*
*a pound of lead*

# FIVE

*a pound of feathers,*
*a pound of lead*

# ELEGY WRITTEN IN MONTPARNASSE

It was August by the time I got around
to holding memorial services
for Ernest Hall Hemingway
who had died in Idaho
where the Styx is called the Snake.

These services were of my own devising
and were held daily for a week
in the Select, the Dome, the Coupole, the Rotonde,
along the Boulevard Raspail,
and on one occasion across the river
under more opulent trees in the garden of the Ritz,
which — it says in English — is reserved
for guests of the hotel.
    *The Snake runs swift in Idaho*
    *and broad through greenest hills.*

This last made me split a gut
because present were Marcel Proust, Edith Wharton,
and the golden, broken man who Christmas died
in Sheilah Graham's ritzy, kindly arms
and lay in the William Wordsworth Room
of a Los Angeles mortuary.
The hotel was so clearly the guest of them
and the obsequies performed by the dead.
    *The Snake swells wide in Idaho*
    *and tumbles bright on rock.*

The Select, the Dome, the Coupole, the Rotonde
were the scene of more homey gatherings

and once the mourners were distracted
by an Arab with a bear upon a chain
who capered upright with a tambourine.
  *The Snake foams white in Idaho*
  *and speckles shale-grey shore.*

Lorn Urania did not appear
nor any sisters of the sacred well,
yet a harmony of dissonance
somehow somewhat loudly swept
the taut, discordant strings.

The Misses Stein, Toklas, Flanner, Beach
assisted at these rites
as well as many others —
S. Anderson, R. Lardner, G. Wescott, T. Wolfe,
M. Twain, Jack London — in general those you would expect,
and although T. Eliot enquired of the waiter,
*"Le service, est-il compris?"*
the others overlooked the breach.
  *The sinuous Snake in Idaho*
  *runs black as blood beneath cold stars.*

Three soldiers from the appropriate war
occupied a table in the not enormous room,
and although I was appalled by the intrusion of a delegation
from Southern California — Ethelbert Nevin,
who yearned to kiss the cross, sweetheart,
and Carrie Jacobs Bond who found a corseted repose
in Forest Lawn's Immortals' Hall — they explained
that it was they who got him his Nobel Prize
and gave him back his middle name.
  *The Snake like snake in Idaho*
  *will freeze to silent winter stop.*

It was a fine company, all in all,
*representative* is the word,

and I thought him laid to decent rest,
though well I knew in Montparnasse
   *That Snake must thaw in Idaho*
   *when aspen trembles coined with spring.*

OPÉRA COMIQUE

(Time Exposure)

The marble eyes
of Ch.-Fr. Gounod
(the brass tag says)

stare from the memorial bust
on a pedestal
in the decorated niche

rounded from paneled
men's room walls
at the Opéra Comique.

The line is long
between-the-acts and moves
intent on troughs

that gurgle counterpoint
of guttural French
to the smoke-blue room.

The shuffling tourist asks
of broadcloth suit
in yellowing stone

(incredulous of arch-assed
cherubim that climb
though winged

the boiled-shirt chest
to finger coyly
   full dress tie)

what Freudian dreams
succeed to Faust
   in aromatic hell?

what moral memories cling,
what nineteenth-century
   pieties

endure in bowered niche
carious with chipped
   plaster where

stubs of rusted wires
bear giltless wraiths
   of dangled marguerites?

# VENEZIA
## (Film Festival)

Cream and chrome the Chris-Craft
cuts the postcard blue
   of waters

drenched with dying dazzle
of Venetian sun
   more gold

within the gilded domes
that fire dusk
   with coppered blaze

than in the darkling sky
where Venus waits
   between twin spires.

     The swath of wake
     careens past palaces
        ornate with marble

     carved to lace, bossed,
     groined, pillared,
        trembling now

     as wash of ancient waters
     folded back
        to swollen foam

     slaps the spittled sides
     of bobbing gondolas
        in wait

until their wrinkled poles
reharden in
the mirrored depths.

So Venice burnished
by the last of sun
trembles, waits

the screen star's
bright arrival at
the Gritti Palace steps

where floodlights tear
the gorgeous rags of day
to sequined tatters

as boathook's brazen "S"
retrieves the Chris-Craft's
cream and chrome.

The manager bows,
the tourist-guests applaud,
and screen star wiggles

(golden underneath
incredible sheath and clutching
cliché poodle)

in a teetered walk
down scarlet carpet,
shedding smiles.

# ROMA

The Via Veneto
is wide, the chocolate
ice cream dark

at the *trattoria* Doney
where Hadrian's boy sits,
new muscled now

from naked marble
into insolence of flesh
contained

in faded blue jeans.

Immaculate with
hyacinthine hair,
he fingers sun

above the molded
plastic table top
and quiet waits

with depth of haunted glance
the antique regard
that yields to life

lost imperial eyes.

# FIRENZE

There are expensive
restaurants along
   the bat-brown Arno

which flows in bluer,
awninged light among
   the goblets, knives,

gold-rimmed plates,
silver wagons holding crimson,
   vein-skinned plums,

green, soft-haired figs,
iced black grapes,
   and rises then to wash

the glint of lustres
hung from ormolu
   chiseled

into gilded vines.
Liquid there the flow
   of Arno quivers

(waiters bring us melons,
wet-rose scampi,
   topaz wine)

in reflective, shimmered light
of tourist afternoon
   dissolving

what is left from
morning's black and grey
    encounter with

the sculptured dead
Medici quick within
    their death-dimensioned tomb.

# ELEGY WRITTEN ON THE LEANING TOWER

The only thing
of any conceivable Utility
that I learned
in the Army Navy
Marine or Air Corps
        was
How to Strip a Butt.

In Florida Kansas
Arkansas Georgia
Shreveport, Louisiana
the process was the same:

You twirled the butt
between the fingers
until the hot head
came loose and fell
— if it was night
in a shower of sparks —
to the dust or gravel or grass
of the dried ground.

The voices would go on then
— inner voices, outer voices, it did not matter —
under the alien skies
of preposterous states
while the fingers crumbed
tobacco shreds
(for Lucky Strike Green

had Gone to War)
into nothing.
                Finally
(oh very finally for some)
the paper would be twisted
to a hard and tiny seedlike core
beneath the fingernail
and as you spoke
rolled back and forth
in no particular rhythm
until the thumb would gather it
from beneath the middle finger's
fleshy pocket.

Then you'd shoot it
— nothing, really nothing —
as if it were memorial aggie
or bone-remembered mib
away into the night
to punctuate some
metaphysical point
about God or Woman
or Loneliness or Stars.

The gesture had,
as I said,
a certain Utility
and recommended itself
to all who might otherwise
have had to spend the morning
picking up Butts.

It was an Aid to Reflection
and although Ulysses had long since
become sad Kilroy,
who big-nosed peered

from toilet walls
and public places,
we did not seem to mind.

So far this is anti-poem
as any anti-poet knows
and while a few remarks
on the impossibility
of Stripping
a Filter Tip
might be allowed
to intrude a note
of *où sont les neiges d'antan*
the anti-poet, the true anti-poet
— French Chilean American Dutch —
is not prepared to admit
that History
is as long as it is,
which is very long indeed.

Longer than wars
or the time between wars.
Longer than nights
or the time between nights.
Longer than men
or the time between men.

And this I knew this summer
when I stood at top of Pisa's tower.
The plain blistered with heat and sun,
and scratched in marble dazzle
of that parapet was "Kilroy,"
sad-nosed, bewildered, sure only of
his own existence and the priority
of that existence to
— all anti-poets take flight;

close your eyes with holy dread
for I have drunk the milk of paradise —
essence.

Kilroy was there.
Memorial fingers moved
as once they moved
and had not moved for years:

  I Stripped a Butt
and rolled the paper
to its tiny core,
 gathering it to the quick of nail.

"See," — we looked, my children there
and I from tilted marble height
at those who had not made
the slanted circle's climb
yet waved to us beneath —
"A pound of feathers," was what I said
— the finger shot the pellet out —
"A pound of feathers,
a pound of lead."

# IN HOLY, HIGH MESHED

In January in holy, high Meshed
suspended in the shimmer floated from
the spines of circling mountains whited by
a snow more fine than tarnished dust and powdery
with portent of dissolution past decay
in sky and driest, scarcely moving air,

lay a garden that I walked, far from home.
Sycamore, poplar, aspen rose (you do not ask
the names in holy, far Meshed) to branch
with web of silvered twigs the dilute sky
that does not arch to dome a seen horizon
but reaches out, before the stars, beyond

the mountains bleached by argent distance.
I longed in silent hanging garden (bare
in holy, mute Meshed) for winter wounds
of northern skies gashed rose with ebb of sun
through lower smutched by inky rags of clouds
scudding before a staining wind above

black clutch of sooty fingered elm or thrust —
remembered flame — of sap-sweet maple, for
it does not seem that spring should ever bloom
where almond, peach, lilac, quince bear winter leaves
of unveined gold as if the dome of mosque had shed
a quiet, shadeless gilt on holy, pale Meshed.

# WISE MEN, MAGI, KINGS
## (Elegy Written at Persepolis)

The satrapies of Lion and Sun lie waste.
No cricket chirps from rich-eared corn
thatch-rooted tough in tended fields,
nor frog white-bellied croaks from summer swamp
alive with midge and intermittent plash
of rotted log to dark incessant waters.
And yet, having come to this place, I have thought
of Wise Men, Magi, Kings.

We are not sure, you know, for while
they have their names — Caspar, Balthazar, Melchior —
and rhythmic move in camel-sway with bells
across the powdery plains past Demavand
and Ararat of murmurous doves,
dust, not mist, obscures their state.

Wise Men? On such a journey?
From Orient to West with astrolabe
as guide? Brass, hammered discs
not perfect round and insecure
on wobbly pins? Sold now as paperweights
to tourists in the bazaars?
Wise Men these? Scanners of the Zodiac.

Incantation must have had a part,
we say, and so we call them priests.
Priests — Magi of the Light and Sun
whose altars blazed in bright Persepolis —
enamored now of night and star
but clutching temple treasure all that way.

Gold, frankincense and myrrh —
and so we paint them kings, put Titian crowns
upon their Doges' heads, Vandyke their robes
to ruby satin billowing with liquid shadows,
and Rubens-oil their flesh to sheen
more rich than pearl of Ethiop's ear.

Their state they hold in palaces beneath
the involute arch of gilded roofs which tell
of bloody Saturn bloody eating bloody sons,
of God-besotted Abraham with knife
untrembling at the bird-skin throat of boy,
Sebastian riddled, Sabine women raped,
Leda stilled by swan-throat thrust to thigh.

Come Westerly, oh Orient Kings,
as I thus Easterly have done,
did hashish dream more mystic-cruel
befog the worship of the Sun?

# VOYAGER'S RETURN
## (A Question)

Must must
  succeed disuse
    invading house
      to dilate nostril
        wide agape with breath
          of death made live within
            our blood when we return,
              turn key in door
                and pause as if
within within
  an emptiness had made
    an utter love
      to utter emptiness —
        void voiding void
          upon the vacancy
            of sheeted beds
              above the haze-dust floors —
getting get
  of odorous loneliness
    intent on vast
      incestuous increase
        immense with threat
          to augurous heart
            stilled so to stop
              at shadowed,
                foot-worn sill?

# SIX

*beyond similitude*

# SIX

*beyond similitude*

# CONVERSATION

*What, is Horatio there?*
*A piece of him.*


"I regret,"
      said Mr. De Paolis
      who spoke so very well
      and who could time
      the surging talk to meet
      the peak of swell,
"The chaos of certainty.
I cannot spend myself
Beyond myself."
          no wave crashed,
          so deep the sea,
          but flotsam, jetsam,
          the green-brown kelp
          and many marine creatures
          subsided beneath
          the new sucked valley
          to seethe within
          the taut and liquid surface.
"You expect,"
      said the other
      who had ventured
      from himself amazed
      but who could hear
      the desperation which
      the mind had phrased,
"To find the psyche
Within — within — the ego?"
          suspended hung the flotsam,
          the jetsam, the knotty kelp

bright with ooze;
light shifted
on the many marine creatures
but slack now
the once taut and silky surface.
"Why not? my potbellied friend,"
said Mr. De Paolis
who hoped with words he could deny
the manumission of heart
which voice would otherwise imply,
"The libido's brew
Must itself renew,
For ego fathers ego."
the flotsam, the jetsam,
the loosened kelp
obeyed no life
but seismic circumstance
but the many marine creatures
in cosmic madness swam
against the impending doom.
"Consider the id!
Consider the id!
That witch's cauldron
Has no lid,"
so the other
who in darkened room
on pallet narrow
had learned that love
was not relief
when sense the senses
still could harrow.
"Oh, my flat-bellied friend,
Narcissus, even pale Narcissus
Had his pool, and thus became
Enamored of a watery twin."

wine-dark the sea
by sudden cloud beclouded
enpurpled with a dye
by air engendered
as element with element contended
to shadow forth
inchoate circumstance.

"It's all done with mirrors?"
                said Mr. De Paolis
                who was quick at the grotesque
                and knew the value to the truth
                of sudden, nut-house arabesque.
"Naked before a sheet of glass
My eyes assess the boundaries
Of this, my hair-fringed flesh?"
                the cloud became a spreading
                stain on water, quenching
                liquid light with flow
                of deep pollution.
                Salt the sea and bitter
                as it moved unmoved
                beneath that sudden night in day.

"Oh bleed, my young friend,
Bleed bright blood,
Or mirrored flesh
Will flesh itself
And bloat with loathing —"
                very grand now, the other,
                oblivious of the spume-flecked sea
                where feathered arms, intent on foam,
                sought form denied immensity —
"The eyes your eyes have seen — and uglied —
Have also seen the burled catalpa loose
Its blooms to melt in pollen-laden air

Before their tissued husks
Dissolve in faintest yellow stain
Upon the skinny, naked heels
Of wanton boys
At summer play."
            open, open now the other —
            the naked mind whose voice was breath —
            to iron scorn, to scalding hope
            that he might save a poet death.
"The eyes your pen has seen, see you,
And seeing you, must see themselves:
The mirror of the aching flesh
Is other flesh, not glass."

  Black were the depths where convoluted shells
  gave up their nacreous splendor to the force
  of swollen waters, leaving pulpy life
  to cling in torn and bloodless remnants
  where liquid rock, which flowed as lava once
  down olive festooned slopes, had suffered change of old
  to labyrinthine caves of unveined basalt cold.

# MR. DE PAOLIS AND THE SHADES

*Eros, ho!*
*The shirt of Nessus is upon me.*
ANTONY AND CLEOPATRA, IV, xii

Of all the blood Ulysses shed
with his broad sword to clot the parched
and during dust of storied plain
or flow in dilute crimson through
those far refracting sky-impacted seas
where thought like restless dolphin
darts with gleaming back to breed,
he could not spare a little cup
for those poor shades who cried aloud
to feel again — remembered pain?

Those shades are at me now for life
and I am no Ulysses who
could stand upon the bourne of world
to shake a brine-encrusted beard
in high rebellion at the graveless dead,
but am suppliant myself
whose one day's stubble with due rite
is sacrificially removed
before a porcelain altar
by priest emasculate in Jockey shorts.

And yet, what blood my flesh has shed
has been my own — the skin drawn taut
across the Adam's apple bleeds
a scarlet thread which seeps
vermillion wet into the white
compressed and manufactured foam
of tiled Cimmerian shore

where mute tears curd in throat
constricting utterance
before an image-crowded glass.

Such easy blood is not for shades
however smeared who thus implore
with lip-begotten lips from nether world
the cup to make their pain immortal;
they will not take the razor's nick
but tear away with claws, which grow
instinct with life as excrement of death,
those analgesic scabs which Time
has laid upon the ulcered flesh
as anodyne.

    And this I know
for I have bled a deeper blood
with fox at nibble in my gut —
such blood flows black as tar
and sweety thick is flushed away
as bitter waste or spewed in gagging
terror to towels held before
the flooding nose and mouth a-tremble
with the sour smell of death.
White enamel pans designed
for sickbed use succeed such towels
and hold the cup the shades entreat,
for this the blood of their desire
and this is blood of mine.

If I were thus to grant them blood
in act of love from my poor store,
massaging heart to fill their gaping
veins insatiate of life,
what would become of me?
Well I know the avarice

of fleshless flesh which feeds upon
the mind of poet in travail
demanding that he live again
odors, sights, attitudes,
inflections of the long-mute voice
whose laughter once was song.

Recall, recall. Total recall.
Must I recall to bleed again
as once I bled those many dawns
I left a semen stainèd bed
to walk across a college town,
a once great prince reduced to stub
of sticky thickened skin amid
my still bedewed and sentient loins?

The girl I left to face those dawns
alone and whom I used as if
she were a moister hand, no more,
is long since dead — her aunt
told me the story at a dinner once,
how rich the man she married
and how they all would miss her.

Mine eyes dazzle; we died young.
Through such dazzle must I look
to limn two shades to suffer still
affrighting eyes and my own soul?
Such costive cormorant recreate
to spend again without surrender?

Lust will lust itself profane
when driven so to re-ennerve
the ache of arms which sought to glut
with simple greed immortal longing.
The blood of tar is blood of tar
in sacerdotal belly transubstantiate.

Has chaos then a history?
Is repetition narrative?
No, I am man and know behind
this Jacobean rant the final
quiet sadness so profound
no liturgy has been devised
to give it form and symbol.
The shades, like worm of Nilus,
shall be given desperate suck,
"Time itself," they whisper,
"You may cheat through us."

Well I knew at twenty summers
what it was to love in truth —
with hand, eyes, nose, tongue, cheek,
and dearest lips enlipping lips,
and very life with life conjoined.
And thus I loved, endowing all
the flesh with every grace and beauty
in the world as after love I looked
into those yielded eyes
which had become my own.

But let me tell you how as once
in June we lay upon a beach
and watched the last thin clouds of smile
dissolve in air with day, we saw
a rolling swell of sea all drenched with gold
as if it held the heart of light
from all the days that we had known
make towards the shore which flickered then
awash with dusk upon the breathing dark.

Oh, it was some trick of shadow
or refraction of an afterglow
upon the cooling dunes, no doubt,
but as the swell met sands of shore

it did not foam but poured its molten
splendor in regift of suns
upon our bodies there —
which cast no shadow —
but were gilt with immortality.

Gold, gold, golden were we then
for the longest moment of our time.

The shades have won; they always win;
you cannot cheat the shades and live,
for living man must speak to love
and loving, he must speak to live.

So tongueless shades cry out to us —
from misted mirror above a knob marked "Waste" —
to ride again the dolphin's back
through no enameled sea
but impact deep in far refracting glass
they ask the anguish of our choice.

They know what blood is ours to shed
and will not cease without their cup.
They tempt us on through joy instinct
in limbs of man who knows the might
of proud renewal in his flesh —
however stained the one-time bed,
however black the sacrificial blood.

Through might of shades I could enpeople me
a world to speak with most miraculous organ
on other shores of worlds unborn where shades,
my only sons, from shadows shall emerge erect
with other blood and mine commingled thus
to rebeget in act of kindred love
a world of such dimension and such scope
as love itself in nisus dares to hope.

# TRIPTYCH

## (Variations on a Theme by Freud)

Just as a planet circles around its central body while at the same time rotating on its own axis, so the individual man takes his part in the course of humanity's development as he goes on his way through life. But to our dull eyes the play of forces in the heavens seems set fast in a never-varying scheme, though in organic life we can still see how the forces contend with one another and the results of the conflict change from day to day. So in every individual the two trends, one towards personal happiness, and the other towards unity with the rest of humanity, must contend with each other; so must the two processes of individual and of cultural development oppose each other and dispute the ground against each other. This struggle between the individual and society, however, is not derived from the antagonism of the primal instincts, Eros and Death, which are probably irreconcilable; it is a dissension in the camp of the libido itself.

Sigmund Freud, *Civilization and Its Discontents,*
Trans. by Jean Rivière (London, 1930), pp. 135–136.

### I

### Image and Syntax

as planet circles round its sun
in circle thus encircling light
ensphered in sphere immutable
succeeding day succeeds its night

while day is driven through the skies
as planet circles round its sun

in spaceless time confined to track
in timeless space to measured run

our days to years to eons spin
impact in centrifuge unending
as planet circles round its sun
fixed in motion bent unbending

from recrement of day in afferent night
cruel-kind our kind-cruel dreams are spun
Icarus lashed to Ixion's wheel
as planet circles round its sun


## TRIPTYCH
## II

### Glance
### (An Imploded Ode)

Piss-proud he
who wished to be
let fly at Ixion's wheel
where Icarus, I,
was hung to dry
by hairy balls from reel.

A stench arose
to ream the nose
as acrid amber stream
hit white hot hoop
which lashed in loop
and piss was hissed to scream.

But Ixion, I,
that I, I eyed
as excrement exploded
on whirring rim

in Tartarus dim
where recrement imploded.

For aye am I
with eye eneyed
to peer through proud ammonic mist;
unhouseled bone
were else alone
had eyes not looked to eyes and kissed.

## TRIPTYCH
## III

### Last Rose of Summer

From curl in seed of acrid hip
the rose in whorl ascends to bloom
envialed in its heart it holds
pistil, stamen — phallus, womb.

Androgynous and self-contained
its odor, texture, shade arise
from out such sweet necessity
as in volute perfection lies.

Let drowse of bee and bottle fly
buzz drunken requiem of rose,
the sequent deaths of man I'll sing
who incomplete completeness knows.

The blowsy rose knows not our need
to burst in joy the whorl of sense
and find beyond similitude
a liquid ease in difference.

# SEVEN

*the holy shudder*

# SEVEN

## *the holy shudder*

# MOUSE HOUSE

Throw-A-Way Mouse Trap. Mouse is lured into pre-baited, pre-set Mouse House where he's caught, killed and contained — all inside the box. Then simply throw away the box, mouse and all! Madam's fingers will never touch the varmint. (Ladies will welcome this!) Modern, sanitary, safe, sure. 6 for $1.29.

*— Advertisement in Sunday Supplement*


Madam will appreciate the convenience.
Ladies will welcome this, for fingers
need not touch corpse, nor affrighted eyes turn
from sudden death in trap by broken back
with tear of blood and greed surprisèd eyes,
a limp tail trailing.

No, madam, those fingers need not touch death,
nor nails incarnadined with Apple Rose
or Cherry Ripe or Hidden Dawn trembling
pluck back the spring sprung bar of high amaze,
for mouse is lured, we will not guess at how,
to Mouse House — pre-baited, pre-set
(cunning domestic counterfeit contrived!)
and he's caught, killed, and therein contained
(oh how modern, sanitary, safe and sure!)
all inside the box, Homemaker,
the Mouse House.

Who would not beat a path through so wide a world
to such a door, six for a dollar twenty-nine?

But the Scotch plowboy, madam, is more in mind
than Sage of Concord, and "fear" is his last word.
I would have you fear now alive,
for death is not for the dead, you know.

What use will you have for such commodity
once we have laid corroded flesh to earth?
And yet those nails will grow excarnate
across your sinking breast as coal-tar silk
of coffin lid in silence rots and droops
in yellowed tatters above those sightless eyes;
nor will it stir of any breath from such
as you who disemboweled, enbalmed will lie
on foam rubber, quilted by machine
to satin stars.

Tremble, madam, tremble yet awhile
for you will not tremble dead nor know
a need for death among the many dead.
As concrete swells to crack in frozen damps of earth
and silvered metal rusts to ash with brownish time,
then white-mouthed worms will death invade
and trailing sticky spittle cross, recross
and cross again to re-envein such flesh
to feed successive generations quick
with viscid spawn.

The Mouse House! Does it not give you pause?
Were it not better to look on death alive?
Ay, the living have deep need of death,
though the dead will know it not, so teeming they
with life which still must feed upon itself
in senseless ravin of the pullulate earth.

I do not ask obsequious tear of you,
nor would I obsecrate such prolonged rites
for varmint caught in act of appetite
as children grant when first they come upon
the goldfish bloat at top of dime-store bowl
and see faint grey of filament unraveled
from the skein of burnished life which floats along

in death above mock depths of room-warm
tropic seas where coral castle wreathed
in water plants still glistens in the sun,
or improvise when singing bird, now mute,
is found in morning stiff on littered floor
of wire cage, claws in air, excrement,
hulls of eaten grain and gravel strewn
in memorial chaos with only cuttlebone
remaining sure, permanent and awaiting other
beak to peck.

We need not, ladies all,
look upon these deaths as children do,
preparing match box with velvet scraps
for fish and bird, nor dig with silver tablespoon
a grave among the roses brave with hungry June,
but we should some element of mystery admit.

No Mouse House, madam, I beg. The garbage can,
the compost heap will do for household thief,
but look upon that broken back,
those greed-surprisèd eyes unclosed at close,
that dark tear of blood, with wonder and decent awe.
Do mouse, I pray, the reverence of revulsion,
the homage of disgust due such trapped life;
let excarnate nails unspring the spring sprung bar
and loose its burden to more spacious air
while madam pays the holy shudder life demands
before the ritual washing of her priestly hands.

# THE FROZEN MEN

Some were caught on the mountain top:
they never had a chance at all,
paralyzed at the fall
of shadows from the Titan rocks
across the sun when the winds stopped.
    *the cold feet cold as any stone*
    *and on up up colder than any stone*

Some felt somehow they had a chance
plodding across scooped plain,
but the drenching rain
froze ache to glaze of cold
and left them brittled glass.
    *the cold thighs cold as any stone*
    *and on up up colder than any stone*

Some sat huddled within the house
awaiting seep of spreading freeze
to come upon and seize
the clay and straw of mortared bricks
and crawl along the walls and floors.
    *the cold groin cold as any stone*
    *and on up up colder than any stone*

Some few head downwards lay in wombs,
conceived before the death of birth
when beating hearts on earth
came to slow and silent stop.
These too perished in the cold.
    *The cold heart cold as any stone*

# CORPSE SONG

They carried me out, the not old man,
   they carried me out of church,
not shoulder high as Housman's lads
   but careful not to lurch

when down three steps the six of them
   unused to quiet weight
shuffled their suburban feet,
   contemplative of fate.

The undertakers helped them lift
   the bronze to chrome-bright track
which drew me from their limp suede hands
   to sun-smeared Cadillac.

"The hearse will pay the tolls," they said
   and did not think it odd
that pennied eyes no longer fee'd
   a fingered river God,

or they should travel sixty miles
   to Howard-Johnson town
and leave the road by the clover leaf
   to set me stilly down:

where spade cut white roots dangling back
   to wait expected guest
and tight rolled turf will blanket soon
   the hairy-nippled chest

long used to swell with greening spring
  at bladed tuber's rise
when late snow feathers waning day
  and melts on lid lashed eyes.

# ANTIPHON

(For Mr. De Paolis and Soprano)

*Si mes vers avaient des ailes
Comme l'oiseau.*
>All the birds at morning lay
>dead upon the beach
>and they strewed the reach
>of rain-ridged sands with beaten death.
>
>Cloud-crushed they lay
>plummeted from sky to wave
>that bore the drowned, the migrant dead
>to graveled sands of shore.

*Si mes vers avaient des ailes
Comme l'esprit.*
>Oh the bodies of those birds
>hollowed at the height
>of blind soar by night
>which starless held enclose of close.
>
>Shard-pierced the shriveled lungs,
>webbed muscles rent, the wings
>storm-frayed in final flex
>of desperate aspiration splayed —

*Si mes vers avaient des ailes —*
>Wind-husked they stir,
>wreathed in wraiths of drying spume
>as breath of dune-dawn creeps through craw
>to quicken quill-bright death.

*Si mes vers avaient des ailes*
*Comme l'amour.*

> Cry caw crow. Raucous
> carnage screech
> across the charnel beach
> where dreamless move
> the bleaching dead.
>
> Raven ravin brave bird heart
> from brittled cage of bone
> which else had fed a resinous rot
> of twig and spore-spent cone.

# CHINOISERIE

(Mr. De Paolis Long after Gautier)

Larger far than wind-blast branch
of scrub-pine twist and rootless
   there
          on grit of yellowed glaze of vase
          pit with pock and staggered hawked
          from staggered piles of boxes stacked
          in Shopping Plaza SuperMart
   where
          young unlovely amble wives
          in slop of counter-broken flats
          and wrinkled shorts
          insinuate with crawl
          of crinkle to crotch
mock bird — not mocking thrush
nor swallow, robin, cormorant, wren —
out of drawing sings no silver song
but ill remembers chime and gong
of mandarin reverberate
through Time and mountains
echoing still with rock-rush streams
and dim interior hush that breathes
a silence visible as pluck
and tremulous whine of unstruck lute
voicing voiceless madrigal
of fall from height of smokey waters
vaporous now in distant rise.
   Here
          Muzak fills the popcorned air
          with twitch of boney rump

at stir on perch of stool
where flakes the sweat-sod leatherette
in fingered smear of clamping chrome —
for dime, the plastic rocking horse
massages infant groin
while mother cokes in sad brassière.

Theophile, God-lover, you,
dare I turn the vase to look upon
the travesty of Chinese Princess there?
Not Yeats-envisioned emperor's toy
of hammered twist Byzantine gold
but once enveined, ennerved, entongued —
hollowed intricate to housel man?
Imperial concubine!
Incomparable artifact!
Necessity made sloe-eyed song!
   Yet
         bound those feet with linen strip —
         bird bones stunt to stub —
  there
         beneath the willow
         and resonant blow of flowering peach.

# MARCH BEACH

Thin swift gull cuts winter twilight sky
with glide to flat-topped picnic rocks
where summer lie the hungry young to love
    (Latex crippling knees in cautious haste,
    the wild heart fearing sudden cop torch
    sweeping stoney shadows naked back from night
    and stars with leer of sniggered swath).

Gull feet plastic-yellow scud the beach
with beady peer of famished eye as bill
pecks pluck of Hershey wrapper bleeding
brown to brittled white of other side.
    (How deep the tremble then with tears
    salt licked with trickle tongued to mouth
    in open twitch of pant retaking air and pain
    before memorial kiss pressed soft
    in moment's thanks to taken breast that pulls
    with tender cling from cheek new-stubbled
    after wait of sun-drenched day.)

Emaciate with winter lack
gristled bone twists gnarl to plunge
ascending swoop without a cry above
the scarcely lapping lake already greyed
with depth to deeper dark than windless shore
or umbered reach of far receiving sky.

# MARCH GARDEN

Pain claws clutch of past in heart
that sudden leaks with runny warmth
when naked arch of elm unghosts
new spring with tremulous bud
not bud but blur in curd-clot sky.
    Cats in wait, wait purchased suet
    tempted birds in Max Schling feeder
    set in lees of soot-smutch'd snow
    (postpaid; redwood will not rot
    but plastic buckles yellow after freeze.)

So many years ago, why now?
To touch to quick too quick for thought
and sudden hot with welt of tears
I could not weep when weeping might
have runneled scald through sear of shock.
    Look earthward, angel, to winter mulch
    of leaves I raked in fall to stand
    of wild sweet peas that tangled fence,
    whose empty pods small sparrows pecked
    when after spill the lipped gash dried.

Oh, I was breathless then in reel.
How assess this agony with that?
The living savor death in mock
to taste its coming; how savor muck
of unmocked mock remembered?
    Fingered hands from boney wrists
    blue-veined with suppling pulse

will pull the winter strew from roots
when March is blown north to woods
that lichenous wait brief summer birds.

Grief flutters winged awhile
as if the breast were careful hand
about a fallen bird whose fear
beat senseless thrash of terror
taut in thin, blued skin.
  Cat, pounce. These cardinals I feed
  are more domesticate than I
  who empty trash with rubbers on.
  No hawk will gut them in such middle flight
  as bloods his claws upon my lights.

# SANDS STREET, BROOKLYN

*All poets (old and new)*
*are always*
*and forever*
*Crossing Brooklyn Ferry*
    *(although they may,*
    *at no extra cost*
    *to themselves or us,*
    *also use The Bridge).*


*But the point is*


*that good poets, the very best,*
*the vintage bards,*
*never get to the other side*


*Where Sands Street is*


*And this makes*
*all poets (old and new)*
*always and forever*
    *(whether they use The Bridge*
    *or Ferry)*
*very difficult for wives*
*or children or anyone else*
*to live with.*

Flesh leans not negligent ever,
Crossing Brooklyn Ferry:
　　Where Sands Street is
　　and lies before the Navy Yard
　　(as I ride the Ferry,
　　going back to then,
　　coming forward into when
　　but I cannot land there now, again)
where sailors — ninety bucks for tailor-mades —
retched dry from gut the dregs of drunks
and pools shone opalescent vomit
under all-night neon splattered,
dimming Gatsby-green with sea-dawn East
and fading moon that held the tide
with loosened fingers.
　　　　　　　　　　(Music by Kurt Weill.)


T. S. to you, oh Thomas Stearns,
with antique taxi throbbing, waiting,
consider throb of waiting ship
awaiting dawn and tide and trembling men.
Ashen then such violet hour,
ashen then the hollowed men.
Send not a blind Tiresias to look
but look with me with eyes that see
what eyes on Ferry must remember.
I would show you fear enfleshed in flesh
not ever husked by lusted lusts,
not ever come to metaphoric dusts.
Phlebas, your Phoenician lies
beneath the warm Icarian sea
where fantailed goldfish shimmering mouth
to nibble chalk-white music from
the pretty zither of mere merchant's bones.

Such man sailed not zig-zag course
through Arctic seas of Murmansk run
nor felt great piston plunge precise
to heart in spurt of blood he had
thought spent in ooze of final night
before his death began again with slip
from swelling tide in lap of shore
to shuddered engines deep with pull.

Fear licked not what was left of heart
while winches screamed geared terror's shriek
beyond the ravenous cries of gulls
awaiting windward garbage flung
in earnest of the torn, young dead
(ninety bucks for tailor-mades)
afloat upon the ocean floor
behind iron-bolt compartment door.